THE BURIED HOUSES

THE BURIED HOUSES

by David Mason

ACKNOWLEDGEMENTS
Some of these poems have appeared in the following periodicals: *The American Scholar*: "The Thing Worth Saving"; *Boulevard*: "Explorations" and "A Textbook of Navigation and Nautical Astronomy"; *The Colorado College Bulletin*: "Disclosure" and "The Next Place"; *Crosscurrents* : "Blackened Peaches"; *Cumberland Poetry Review*: "The Old Brit," "In the Physic Garden" and "To a Photojournalist"; *Hellas*: "Recipe"; *The Hudson Review*: "Spooning"; *The Literary Review*: "Small Elegies"; *North Dakota Quarterly*: "Gusev"; *Poet Lore*: "Journal and Prayer" and "The Catch"; *Poetry*: "In the Islands"; *The Sewanee Review*: "The Feast of the Rose Garlands"; *Sequoia*: "At the Graves of Castor and Pollux"; *Soundings East*: "Colloquy in Seattle" and "The Mountain Climber"; *Southwest Review*: "A Map of Scotland"; *Williwaw*: "Dry Granite" and "Summer Nights."

A limited edition of "Blackened Peaches" was published by Aralia Press.

Some of these poems have appeared in a chapbook entitled *Small Elegies* and published by Dacotah Territory Press.

Book design by Lysa McDowell

Story Line Press
Three Oaks Farm
Brownsville, OR
97327-9718

Publication of this book is thanks in part to the generous support of the Nicholas Roerich Museum, the Andrew W. Mellon Foundation, New York, and our individual contributors.

CONTENTS

For Anne Lennox
And In Memory of Douglas Cameron Mason

I

TO A PHOTOJOURNALIST

Imagine a day no photographs
were taken, all were given back
to the years and places where you found them.
The day events undid themselves
airwaves and bookstores simply blanked
and politicians forgot to posture.
The day you met a newsboy hawking
plain white pages to the crowd's relief.
A way of starting over, seeing
through an undistorted lens.

And what you saw that day would be
the pattern of all days before it,
all fires and accidents, the child
who screams, the passive woman who sits
outside the rustle of the world,
visited by those she buried.
No film or paper could collect
the messages of such a day;
they would inhabit you at last,
a kind of knowledge you would welcome.

THE FEAST OF THE ROSE GARLANDS

(Rudolf II, 1552-1612)

On his bad days he asked to be alone,
locked up with everything that he had saved:
the astrolabes, sheet music, a narwhal's horn,
so many objects, all of which he loved,
wishing he had never been born.

As some keep cats he kept his alchemists,
his phial of dust from which God created Adam,
nails from Noah's Ark, and a homunculus
in alcohol. Kepler and Brahe would roam
his hallways, talking calculus.

But no possession, no idea, no work
of sculpture could prevent his moodiness.
Even his nightingales sensed when he was dark.
Their songs could not preserve him from distress,
nor could a ramble in his park.

Yet there was always something more to own,
something he couldn't bear to be without.
That Dürer, bought in Italy, was one:
Virgin and Christ child, an angel with a lute,
attended by two cherubim,

and all the people bowing to receive
garlands of roses in the Virgin's sight.
So exquisite that he became its slave,
its sky was like a memory of light.
The object had become his love.

Orders were given. A corps of young men
walked across the Alps, through col and gorge,
the peaks above them like an icy heaven
wholly indifferent to their precious charge.
They judged their emperor insane

but never dropped the painting once. At Prague
the great work joined him in his misery.
His secret talks with rabbi, priest and mage
would end, and he would wander off to see
Brueghels and Titians. Then the urge

would strike him to see the blue behind her throne.
The German's rendering of the Italian hills
was timeless, like the wish to be alone.
But gazed at long, even perfection dulls
like dust above the town at noon.

THE THING WORTH SAVING

in memory of Bruce Chatwin

I had your postcard from the Volga River
and envied you the life of worn-out boots,
the way you exercised ideas by walking.
Pascal wrote, "Our nature lies in movement,"
but restlessness was more your realm than his.
What fine object, distilled or framed, collected,
cherished for its patina, would you have chosen
to keep? What voice, what face would finally
express the thing worth saving? I met you
waiting for a bus eight years ago in Greece,
one stop in an exhaustive string of places
keyed to the eccentric, to hate and love.

Starting from your grandmother's where you saw
the hide of mylodon inside a cabinet,
and Sotheby's, eyes darkened by appraisal,
you knew how damning our perfection is.
We are the ones who settle and destroy,
build and regret, wishing we could leave it,
wishing the code would signal our migration.
To get out of a car, thank the driver
and sling the moment's household on your back,
looking ahead at open roads and fields
no crows darken. . . .

                    Your life and lines are free,
your voice takes on the rhythm of your steps.

COLLOQUY IN SEATTLE

Today there is nothing that we need to do
but meet with friends. "The sun is nudging me
outdoors," one of us said, and so we have
been sitting for hours on Melinda's deck,
discussing words and looking out at mountains.

Michelle declares that words are merely flags
commanded by a troop of generals,
mostly male. Father Howell attaches them
to a dead Bishop of El Salvador,
mourns that country long without a savior.

Meanwhile, the sun has crossed to touch Michelle's
left shoulder—I could say like a jealous lover—
and Carl opines that words create an emptiness
where empty people meet. Yet what we say
could be said to have a kind of conviction.

Richard, the journalist in our small crowd,
leans forward: "Once I was stood against a wall
in Lebanon, by four young men with guns.
I didn't understand a word they said.
Their AK-47s could have come

from anywhere. It struck me that in minutes

I could be in someone's photo essay,
a grisly exemplar, and then I thought
How silly to be that kind of corpse
with one shoe off, and perhaps a blotch

of gore where I used to have a smile. Maybe
they would make the dead American a cause,
maybe I would be that nameless thing
you hear about in films of World War II,
lost in a rubble no one comprehends."

The pale blue mountains floating out at sea,
almost disappearing in a drift of clouds,
remind us here the world is relatively calm,
intact and clean, the work of talented surgeons
who close their wounds precisely and forever.

Words are wounds, too, I say to myself,
but I'm too tired for explanations.
Today it should be enough to be with friends
and feel all arguments abate in sunlight,
as if it were a rare and precious thing.

GUSEV

from the story by Anton Chekhov

The wind has broken free of its chain.
The sea has neither sense nor pity,
and what befalls us falls like rain.
The water's hot as new-made jelly.

The sea has neither sense nor pity.
One dies while playing a game of cards.
The water's hot as new-made jelly.
Above it there are curious clouds.

One dies while playing a game of cards.
Pavel insists he is getting well.
Above the ship are curious clouds
like lions leaping over the swell.

Pavel insists he is getting well
and dies still hating the peasant class.
Lions leaping over the swell
turn to scissors as they pass.

He dies still hating the peasant class
while Gusev lies in a fevered state.
Clouds turn to scissors as they pass
and dead men find it hard to hate.

Gusev lies in a fevered state,
wishing he didn't have to die,
and though he finds it hard to hate
he's saddened when he sees the sky.

Wishing he didn't have to die,
he goes below to suffocate,
saddened now he's seen the sky.
He thinks of snow, the village gate,

and goes below to suffocate,
his dreams increasingly absurd.
He sleighs through snow, the village gate,
sleeps two days, dies on the third.

His dreams increasingly absurd,
he tosses the fever from his bed,
sleeps two days, dies on the third.
They sew the sail-cloth over his head.

He tosses the fever from his bed.
The fever smiles and crawls back in.
They sew the sail-cloth over his head.
Below deck someone's dying again.

The fever smiles and crawls back in.
The wind has broken free of its chain.
Below deck someone's dying again,
and what befalls us falls like rain.

EXPLORATIONS

from a line by Hart Crane

Compass, quadrant and sextant contrive
to circumnavigate the known
as mapped by sailors who survive
questions they impose.

Others, sailing with similar flags,
sink beneath the obvolute waves
and break apart. The water drags
their deadweight bodies down.

Broken, they discover islands
scattered in archipelagoes
that arch across the summer doldrums
and bridge the winter snows.

Drowned flesh goes sallow or grey.
Flags of peeled flesh wave
with coral lungs. The sea-worms prove
more than the sailors say.

THE OLD BRIT

I sit at my usual waterfront cafe
and watch the youth of Germany invade
with money and Minoltas, buying ruins.
The walls that time decays they reinvent;
Greece will sell herself in order to survive.

I know they gave us Goethe, Schiller, Bach,
but I can't abide their voices in this climate.
I was here for the retreat, you know. Our tanks,
rusty as old tins, fell apart on the roads.
We left the guns pointing north, a ploy

against superior barbarians,
and jammed the quay at Monemvasia.
I remember one old Greek who'd been at Smyrna
cried when the Union Jack went down. The others
shut themselves inside their homes and waited.

Then Crete. The sky blossomed with German chutes,
the flower of Hitler's youth picked off
like so many clipped geese, or stoned by peasants
the moment their boots hit earth. So many.
The Fuhrer could afford to send them all.

My war was a series of bungled retreats
and sun-dazed battles in North Africa,
every lull an impromptu cricket match.
Now when the simoom blows from Libya
the gritty air carries a desert stench,

gardens planted early wilt in the heat.
Above the grey Mediterranean's
frothy, bullying waves, I feel my past
rise like anger from that southern furnace,
monotonous bellow that leaves a bitter taste.

I have made too many errors, and find
I've become a sort of caricature,
the old Brit drinking by the Grecian shore,
singing sunset numbers from the music hall,
rehearsing lies about women from Hong Kong.

DAPHNE

Now that you have come down
the marble footpath to the sea
there is more to choose.
You could ride the bus north to precipitous gorges,
go south with the fruit vendor
calling out on his megaphone
to any lover chance may bring.

Your feet formed to stones and thin sandals,
you could walk as far as it takes to recite
the few dead lines you remember,
each pebble a syllable
turned over, past uttering,
like your lovers' names.

Here white houses put tiled heads together,
deflecting sunlight.
You pause dryly
and choose the small cafe by the quay
where men sit at blue tables
worrying beads and glancing at your legs.

The waiter brings you water.
You let it stand,
a very stasis in a glass.

You cannot get enough of it,
the taste of cistern
like a secret carved in the stone.

Then coffee, medium sweet.
Its demitasse makes you feel a giantess,
laurel turned woman
now that the hunter's gone.

Yesterday at this same table
a German long in the village
showed you the patterns left in your cup.
"The Greeks, they believe it jokingly."
A man with his arms outstretched
came toward you in the rim, but you turned away
to the shapes that looked like goats
or four-legged chickens with udders.
You were the one clasping snakes.
"It is charming, yes?"

It has been too long
since your veins gripped the earth,
now spiny and scantily blossomed.
In the hills there were cool gullies
enclosing gardens; here
the sunlight, with its longevity,
flatters everyone.

It is charming, yes.
But it is not your country,
nor have you ever gone crying
into the arms of a goddess.

THE BONE HOUSE

I can't recall which saint they named the church after,
only that its door was locked, its ikons hidden, its
       tiles and gargoyles
blunted by winter storms or the fierce, solitary and
       persistent sun,
all that was left a fine dry grit I felt with my hand.

Six or seven houses buckled under the evil eye, or
       indifference, I don't know which.
In one, a lace curtain hung, pale and delicate,
gracing its window. Over the stiff grass and scrub
       oak,
cicadas like mad inheritors scraped the air.

It was a long walk up to the village. I stood in my
       jacket of sweat, gazed along the slab
to the stone ring where graves lay in the grass, some
       open, and beside them
the bone house leaned like a disused shed in a dry
       garden.
There in another life the dead were visited, their
       bones washed and sorted in small boxes,

sometimes decked with flowers. There you could meet a
       woman you had known

reduced to a white grimace, her grave passed to new
      tenants in three-year leases.
The earth held no one long, gave them back to their
      names and families,
and death was no more secretive than sunlight in an
      olive grove.

But there I found the boxes opened, the skulls of
      strangers spilled in a mockery of coversation,
the ringing heat of the air that was their scream.

THE NIGHTINGALES OF ANDRITSENA

What did my young compatriots think of me,
those fawn-skinned children blond as German beer,
or the dark-haired ones full of their own freshness?
Did they wonder how I came to live in Greece,
or was I simply Mrs. Finn, translator,
tour guide, sadly middle-aged? As agreed
we met in Athens, and our Arcadian sweep
through history in an air-conditioned bus
began.

      Professor Baird was keen to know
the right way to pronounce Epidauros.
At Nestor's palace he lectured out on the grass,
but those of us who formed his audience
were dazzled by the sea, the fishing boats
caught, it seemed, in pure, unframeable blue.
Though I sat politely, hands in my lap,
the students might have seen I hated lectures.
Perhaps they didn't notice me at all,
and who would blame them? Why should they want to know
one's hair grays, one's husband leaves, one's tongue
turns to stone?

      My children, older than these,
live in America. I have a room

on Skyros facing the sea, a single bed.
I read long books alone just as I did
that night in Chicago many years ago
they came to tell me that my father was dead.

I haven't got a reason for living here,
not a real one. It's better for these students
wanting sunlight and a good rate of exchange.

                    *

For some it's always harder. They want more
but with a vague unease, as I wanted words
to guide me by the solid things they stood for,
held like the tang of wine, tasted like flesh,
as if all time might coalesce, memorable,
firm and rounded by the motion of the sea.

One boy, Ross, was like that. He had come
from a small town near Seattle. Reading books
had given him his first whiff of the world.
I think he was nineteen. I remember thinking
Oh, to be nineteen again, blessedly
empty-headed, able to dream in Greek!
He was the only student on the bus
who wanted lessons; for him the language came
like something his body's motion could inhabit.

A girl named Angela would sit near Ross.

I thought them a couple, as we often do
who watch young people from a distance, guessing
at their lives. Both were good-looking, dark-haired,
with burnished faces, dreamy more than studious.
But he was curious about the world
and that set him apart. Angela, I think
was curious about Ross.

                    We became friends.
The girl joined us at our breakfast lessons,
fumbled with us through the primer, as if
our struggle with words puzzled and intrigued her.
I didn't mind. He wasn't distracted yet.

                    *

We left the seacoast with its olive groves,
its sunlight trellises, baskets of fish
and bougainvillea. Our bus turned inland.
Above Andritsena the temple of Bassae
crowned its grassy mountain, the gray stone
columns cruder than the Parthenon's,
each of them set apart like a new word,
magnificent in mass and workmanship.

After the usual lecture Professor Baird
took most of his charges back to our hotel.
Ross and Angela stayed behind with me;
the keeper showed us how to find the path.

"Walking is good for the heart," the keeper said,
though he was waiting for his cousin's taxi.

Good for the heart, the silence after lectures,
after the last black spume of bus exhaust,
the silence of a walk through oak forests.
Ross was the strongest of us, but held back,
letting me set our pace. He wanted to know
the words for temple, footpath, oak, stream.
Here the trees were large and very old.
We heard the tuneless clatter of goat bells
and saw the shepherd watching from his ridge.

We saw Andritsena from above, came down
as if to land like birds on its tiled rooftops.
The paths were full of woodsmoke, cooking smells
that quickened us. We had come eight miles
in near silence; the chatter of village life
rose slowly as we entered and sat down
under the plane tree by the cistern. Ross
opened the cistern's door, described its room
carved out of rock, full of the cool water.
His voice became two voices, one loud
and hollow like a cave, the other muted,
ordinary, as he withdrew his head and laughed.
But we couldn't linger there. We were late
to meet the others at the tourist hotel.

*

The nightingales won't let you sleep in Platres.

Sitting on my balcony as evening drifted
down from the oak forests, from the strong limbs
of the gray temple, into the gully below,
I had opened my Seferis to that poem.

Won't let you sleep, won't let you sleep. The day
had filled me with its grand foolishness,
being caught up by, of all things, a rhythm.
Won't let you sleep.

                So, you must be thinking,
here comes the epiphany of Mrs. Finn,
the moment when she sees how vain she is,
and you won't be far from wrong. I sat alone,
wondering what they thought of me, but mostly
what he thought, younger than my youngest son.
Hadn't my husband done it, chased the body
of a girl he hardly knew, someone met
at work, a plaything he later bored?

I knew that soon Ross and Angela would come
and we would listen for the nightingales.
The maid had told us there were nightingales
capable of twelve distinctive melodies.
Imagine that—twelve songs by heart, and all
the literary baggage: Keats, Seferis. . . .

I sat there frozen, holding my Seferis
and thinking how they wouldn't let me sleep,
the images, that girl reading her book
in Chicago when they came with the awful news.
I held the book so tightly in my lap
that I had bent its cover.

The children came. I saw that they were children
in spite of their gracous manner with the wine.
They both wore shorts. I admired their brown limbs,
saw the gentle way he touched her hand.

At last we heard the singing from the shadows
of the dark, silent chorus of the leaves.
We listened for the life inside each note,
or rather the children did, Ross leaning
out as if resisting an urge to fly;
Angela, her sense of possibility
untarnished, smiled like an archaic statue.

For me it had all gone flat. I won't deny
the music of the birds was beautiful,
but I saw how we transformed it in our minds
to what we had expected it to be.
I saw the evening's mood envelope them,
how what they had desired became a shell
of words—of empty, captivating words.

It angered me that I would think this way.
I knew that I was spiteful, that the girl
had everything I thought I'd ever wanted,
the thoughtlessness that comes with being young.

Because of who I am, who I've always been,
I know the nightingales won't let me sleep.
I do not think that I have ever been young.
I do not think I have let myself be young.
I am a woman whose father committed suicide
in Chicago in 1939.

RECIPE

For Jon Griffin

With the stately concentration of a priest
you enter your small kitchen and amass
ingredients for the transcendent dinner.
Collops of chicken sauted in olive oil
are set aside to let plain garlic brew.

Onions, deftly chopped, and peeled tomatoes
bubble in oil with olives from Kalamata.
Tonight the only rule is improvise,
but from much reading of the proper texts—
the ones whose authors weigh what they know.

Poetry is so much less forgiving.
The wine we drink tonight speaks straight
from the sun of France,
the crumbled feta you stuff the chicken with
might once have hung from ritual rafters

With luck we will surround this table again,
garnish conversation with a line from Frost
or Yeats' palpable distillations
out of time. But your provision here
no one can publish or repeat.

II

WHAT IS IT THERE?

More than anything, an atmosphere
laden with water, the ice and rock
of peaks that, in the clouds' embrace,
are only memories or myths
exposed in sudden revelations;
a river green with glacial silt
connects them to the frosted farms,
lumberjacks' small towns and taverns'
beer lights glowing in dark windows;
the sound a constant muffled roar
as water falls and ice breaks free,
rising like earth's mist exhalations
from hills bearded with Douglas firs,
falling from the mountain passes,
heather under snow, to woods
no eye can penetrate; the calls
of crow and chainsaw, fishermen
knee deep in the river's clatter—
sounds heard at last as silence
caught in the slow descent of clouds,
the dampness softening all fears.
A mother screams for her lost son
until the walls remember it,
and where there are no walls a crow
clings to its rainy branch, scattering
small drops of water as it takes the air.

VERSIONS OF ECOTOPIA

God help the land that is unlucky enough
to be popular, where everyone wants the view
of islands like loaves and fishes in the west,
the seiner placed just right in the composition,
and rain is gentle as a Japanese scroll.

Perhaps you've been there, remember salmon smoked
on alder coals, or have seen the northern lights
like a drunken cloud off a gillnetter's deck,
and said, "I want to own these stars and davits,
lower my skiff each night in the same dark sound!"

Or was it you who stood inside the dike
and watched the valley heated to a griddle,
the playing field of gulls and combines, cooked
in the flying chaff? You waved your arms, shouting,
"Milkpails, silos, trucks, pallets, fog—all mine!"

Goggled, slogging with ice axe to the glacier,
you watched the comb of Heaven touch the clouds
and make them cry, the blue diadem of ice
reach forever in heart-stopping air, until
you prayed your bones would vanish in this grave.

Mountain, sound or valley clung to you
like sweat in suburbs where you worked and thought.
But others like you dreamed of the Promised Land
and schemed to have Ecotopia, whispering,
"There's more than one way to skin a madrona tree!"

For those who always lived there it was dull
as drive-in movies and hot cars, until
the heroes of development had built
a bit of Phoenix by the oyster beds,
a Trumpish tower downtown, L.A. at the fringe.

As murdered buffalo disturb our dreaming plains,
a rainy fish smell lingers in Ecotopia.
At night the plaid giant rattles his axe
and growls in Swedish, up to his neck in muck
where the tall, unbarbered forest used to be.

You find yourself in unexpected traffic,
pressed in a narrow shoal of weeping lights,
looking through the rain for an exit sign,
and thinking of an old scroll you once saw
rubbed to nothing by a billion loving hands.

IN THE ISLANDS

Parents had gone where parents go,
except for Mrs. Pocket, who sat against a log,
engrossed in a paperback, smoking a Lark
and tugging absent-mindedly
her swimsuit's oily strap.

Our minor wounds stung by dried salt, we were appalled
how far the kelp had been dragged up,
left like silage from a great combine.
Crows hawked in the Douglas firs,
their inland world dense and inaccessible,

so I and the other children stayed on the open beach,
tow-headed, curious and bored.
Some rocks we could overturn, and there
we subjugated neighborhoods of tiny crabs
who scampered from the light.

Between our playing and the woods
the bones of old trees bleached by the Sound
were heaped as if in the aftermath of battle.
I crawled inside a rack of driftwood,
pretending it was home.

By now, insinuating tides have tugged it apart.
Mrs. Pocket finished her book, and sometime later
died of cancer. Her daughters have grown up,
no longer the crabs' tormentors.
We've all been changed,

drifting into new configurations
and seldom taking time to watch the light.
But we remember boredom,
the pleasure of letting days go nowhere
till something called us home.

THE BURIED HOUSES

On maps the sea turns inward from Cape Flattery.
To cross the strait risks fog, absence of all markings.
South of the cape the forest wall is continuous,
or was when I first saw it. We were a family then,

huddled on the beach in the quiet, pattering rain
while daddy-long-legs trawlers bobbed between
          haystacks.
One day we found an anchor left from an old shipwreck,
but mostly I remember the sea was far away.

That year the archeologists began to dig
(an old Makah reported bones jutting from the cliffs),
uncovering the shafts and flukes, floats, coils of line
that lay among the fire pits of an ancient village.

They found a wooden dorsal sequinned with otter teeth,
the terrifying masks that would have called to spirits
whose longhouses lay two hundred fathoms deep.
They found the bowls for salmon, candlefish and
          berries.

Artifact by artifact, they reinvented a buried world
whose dailiness was well-suited to this coast.
They cut into the clay with hoses, washing years
into the sea, drawn down by the puzzle of bone.

Since then, more has changed than I could tell you
        about,
but sometimes I go back to see what they have learned.
Much is known by now about the buried houses,
less about the people who uncovered them.

A TEXTBOOK OF NAVIGATION
AND NAUTICAL ASTRONOMY

Academy approved, this volume stands
among my books of poetry, its spine
erect as an old blue uniform, stiff
inside with yellow, nineteen-forties glue.
I take it down and follow with a finger
charts that date back nearly to Mercator.
Problems here have steps to their solutions.

I see my father decked in Naval whites,
young, red-haired, immaculate, this book
held tight as he crossed Annapolis.
A small-town midwest boy, at twenty-one
he was reading, "Situation: Target ship
on course 010 degrees. . . .Required:
Bearing of target ship when you fire. . . ."

By minutes and degrees my father drew
vectors that would intersect
and finish in imaginary flames.
But that was only school. When it came time
and the ship rang hollow with explosive fire,
when tracers arced to the burning Zero,
nothing he wrote home could stop the horror.

Later, when he left affectionate strangers
who shared his house, and lost the town's approval,
perhaps his skill at navigating saved him.
This book calls Sirius the brightest star,
Canopus next. Remember. The still trees
at night are shadows, uncertain of their limbs.
No one can tell you what to see.

AT THE GRAVES OF CASTOR AND POLLUX

It breaks your back
to consider the stones
men used to bear,
not to mention
their burden of belief.
The constellations
animated

guards against loss,
guiding sailors home.
We are meant to believe
of Leda's sons
that the wrestler was a midget
and lay with his brother
in these chiselled troughs.

Brothers who fought,
scaling Taygetus
on a worn path
above the trees
to the bluest death,
the farthest arch,
Gemini.

I dreamed
a hall light was on,
my own brother
coming to see me
months after he fell.
I was never happier,
shouting his name that was

palpable as a shell.
In the old days
dead men were seen
in the stars,
courses charted,
walls built. . . .
I'll watch tonight.

SMALL ELEGIES

I.

I've had enough of bruised eyes and waiting:
traveling cross-country in one of those
flights of the imagination. But this is real.
He lies in the cool room like an ambushed hero
in the dreary colors of an old photograph.
As if he were turning in sleep, his hands poise
like listless guards before his face.
I watch, and what I cannot finally believe
is that he is not asleep, not moving. He seems
so much himself—even his small smile
and the blood on one of his motionless fingers,
filmed with dirt from the mountain that he climbed.

II.

My brother taught me how
to climb with crampons, cut steps in the ice,
hold him on belay. But in the chimneys
we descended without ropes, otherwise
I would have fallen too.
I called his name as if he were alive,
traversed the hard black face and slid

down a thousand feet in a couloir's glare.
On the glacier I was looking up and looking
into the crevasse. When the helicopter came
I didn't want to leave him, though the stormclouds
rushing out of nowhere forced us from the peak.
Flying out, I watched the darkened snow.
My hands still felt, from earlier that day,
the tension of my brother's weight on the rope.

THE MOUNTAIN CLIMBER

It is not my place to tell what joy
carried you there, though I know
exactly how the body moves upward
to what seems a limitation.

Bear grass, heather, scree. . . .
The bending creek reflects a cloud.
Otherwise this sun-scrubbed clarity
stabbing off the ice.

It is hard to believe the glacier moves,
falling to its own return.
You hear the blue ice crack and tumble,
peeling the mountain down.

From the summit you can see so far:
the polished top of the globe
beneath its vapor trails.
The body is constantly ready

to fall. In another year
you would have turned
thirty, cornered in career,
joking about the suit that didn't fit.

DRY GRANITE

We come to these rocks
with elkhorn-velveted shrubs,
knowing their runnelled expressions
by the roughness at hand.
Rock shoes, rope, hexes and slings
that dangle like nooses.
The pressure in our bodies keeps
our spirits climbing.

It has been ten years since I climbed like this
on dry Colorado granite, under
blue sky, breathing tinder,
terrified, my fingers scraped
to a numb throbbing. . . .
Ten years since I last pretended
a spider's ease with heights.

The canyon is quiet: old November snow
and the motionless granite.
Below us the creek bends darkly,
turning away from the blue.
The mind falls slowly, pressed
like water to absolute clarity.
A magpie watches from the pines.

Watching my brother climb, I am watching
the ghost of my brother
who died climbing.
But we are older, admit to our fear.
The briared jam-crack holds me
bent and trembling in the rock.
The water curving below
washes stones in the sunlight.

AN ABSENCE

My window fills with cidery light,
filtered through a screen of maples
and thickened by the last of summer.
I'm older than you ever were
—that will never be right.

Our blood has altered. Yours was burned
and scattered with your bones and hair
in the mountains. Filtered through my hands,
it fell like snow into the heather.
Everywhere I turned

I felt you rise and fall away
in the blue vertigo of glaciers.
A sudden absence made the firs
and waterfalls more than themselves.
I knew I wouldn't stay.

Now I live in another state
with hills for mountains and less rain.
You would have hated the small scale
of everything here, and how pain
comes early, stays late.

I've grown by distances, and lost
that place where I could visit you.
Though nothing's written on your stone,
I hope you never feel alone.
I hope it feels like rest.

JOURNAL AND PRAYER

We've fixed this study for me with a view
of islands where my children used to play,
the vacant sky reflecting my dark and light.
They say sky's highest particles are ice
and that's what the soul becomes—particles
leaving earth circle by wider circle,
set free at the startled edge of light.

I went to see the Father at nine-fifteen.
We talked as if to keep out of the rain
but soon were lost in stories of our lives.
Father Clark was jailed in China. Today
and often in the past I said I had a son
who traveled through the mountains of the east
and died in mountains—oh, six years ago.

A second son would find me in my room
where with shades drawn tight I cradled gin.
He'd beg me to go outside among the trees
as if a wound could open to the weather,
take rain into its blood and purify
the motions one goes through each dreary day.
I felt I'd bled myself of all desire.

How thoroughly I resisted, though each
empty chair was a presence I knew well,
a space without a body or a voice.
My father died early, my sons' father
left, our marriage burst like a child's balloon.
I found myself in rooms full of echoes.
The light around the curtains hurt my eyes.

The Father had no windows in his cell
but spoke lightly of his Chinese regimen.
After our meeting I walked to a town park,
saw the swings where my children used to play
were empty, the hedges heavy and bent.
They'd drained the wading pool where now light rain
pasted leaves to cement. I walked until the cold
soaked through to my skin, spoke this prayer
for no reason, and without confirmed belief:
All I have lost is fed into these trees;
lighten me, Lord, with your green presence.

A WEIGHT

in memory of Garth Kingsley

The hillsides, packed with fern and alder, hugged
the road and the land's terse edge,
and water permeated everything,
sucked into a billion roots
or lapping, clear and cold, at the lake's far end.

Our playground: terror grown in unnamed places
where the road halts somewhere in woods,
and wooden houses, half indigenous, smoke
gently over their civil gardens.
No one swings on the cedar's knot of rope.

Now that you're gone the line hangs in mid-air.
The trestle over Smith Creek's been
derailed, though I hear one can still find spikes
uncovered where the soil caves in.
We used to collect them in a wooden basket.

The weight is gone. And the aluminum boat
we flipped in a storm? I should know
whether your mother or your widow has kept it.
Looking back at a young man's death
we see the other ways he might have died.

For you it was like every day a day of work,
a simple misstep from a ladder,
a few unconscious hours in the hospital. . . .
For us it was colder, faster
than a flood, intimately wrong forever.

SPOONING

After my grandfather died I went back
to help my mother sell his furniture:
the old chair he did his sitting on,
the kitchen things. Going through his boxes
I found letters, cancelled checks, the usual
old photographs of relatives I hardly knew
and my grandmother, clutching an apron in her hands.
And *her*. There was an old publicity still
taken when she wore her hair like a helmet,
polished black. Posed before a cardboard shell
and painted waves, she seemed unattainable,
as she was meant to.

              For years we thought he lied
about his knowing her when he was young,
but grandfather was a man who hated liars,
a man who worshipped all the tarnished virtues,
went daily to his shop at eight, until
the first of three strokes forced him to retire.

He liked talking. Somebody had to listen,
so I was the listener for hours after school
until my parents called me home for dinner.
We'd sit on his glassed-in porch where he kept a box
of apples wrapped in newsprint.

He told me about the time he lost a job
at the mill. Nooksack seemed to kill its young
with boredom even then, but he owned a car,
a '24 Ford. He drove it east to see
America, got as far as Spokane's desert,
sold the car and worked back on the railroad.

Sometimes he asked me what I liked to do.
I told him about the drive-in movies where
my brother, Billy, took me if I paid.
In small towns everyone goes to the movies.
Not grandfather. He said they made them better when
nobody talked, and faces told it all.
"I knew Lydia Truman Gates," he said,
"back when she was plain old Lydia Carter
down on Water Street. One time her old man
caught us spooning out to the railroad tracks.
Nearly tanned my hide. He was a fisherman—
that is, till she moved her folks to Hollywood."

I don't know why, but I simply couldn't ask
what spooning was. He seemed to talk then
more to his chair's abrasions on the floor,
more to the pale alders outside his window.
The way he said her name I couldn't ask
who was Lydia Truman Gates.

*

                "Nonsense,"
was all my mother said at dinner. "His mind
went haywire in the hospital. He's old.
He makes things up and can't tell the difference."

I think my father's smile embarrassed her
when he said, "The poor guy's disappointed.
Nothing went right for him, so he daydreams."

"Nonsense," my mother said. "And anyway
no Lydia Truman Gates ever came
from a town like this."

                "It's not so bad a place.
I make a pretty decent living here."

My mother huffed. While I stared past my plate
Billy asked, "Who is Lydia Truman Gates?"

                *

It wasn't long before we all found out.
The papers ran a story on her. How
she was famous in the twenties for a while,
married the oil billionaire, Gates, and retired.
She was coming back home to Nooksack. The mayor
would give a big award and ask her help
to renovate our landmark theatre.

Our mother said we had better things to spend
our money on than some old movie house,
though she remembered how it used to look.
She said that people living in the past
wouldn't amount to much.
Billy and I pretended we didn't care.
We didn't tell our parents where we went
that night, riding our bikes in a warm wind
past the fishhouses on the Puget Sound,
and up Grant Street to the Hiawatha.

Inside, Billy held my hand, and showed me
faded paintings of Indians on the walls
and dark forest patterns in the worn carpet.
The place smelled stale like old decaying clothes
shut up in a trunk for twenty years,
but Nooksack's best were there, some in tuxes,
and women stuffed into their evening gowns.
We sat in the balcony looking down
on bald heads, high hair-dos and jewels.
Near the stage they had a twenty-piece band—
I still remember when the lights went out
the violins rose like a flock of birds
all at once. The drums sounded a shudder.

We saw *Morocco Gold, The Outlaw, Colonel Clay*
and the comic short, *A Bird in the Hand,*
flickering down to the screen
where Lydia Truman Gates arose in veils,

in something gossamer
astonishing even in 1965.
Lydia Truman Gates was like a dream
of lithe attention, her dark eyes laughing
at death, at poverty or a satin bed.
And when they brought her on the stage, applause
rising and falling like a tidal wave,
I had to stand up on my seat to see
a frail old woman assisted by two men,
tiny on that distant stage.

My brother
yanked me past what seemed like a hundred pairs
of knees for all the times I said, "Excuse us."
We ran out where the chauffeur
waited by her limousine, his face painted
green by the light from Heilman's Piano Store,
breathing smoke. "You guys keep your distance."

"Is she coming out?"

He crushed his cigarette:
"No, she's gonna die in there. What do you think?"

More people joined us, pacing in the alley,
watching the chauffeur smoke by the door propped
open with a cinderblock.
And then the door half-opened, sighed back,
opened at last on the forearm of a man.

Behind him, Lydia Truman Gates stepped out
with her cane—hardly the woman I had seen
enduring all the problems of the world
with such aplomb. She stared down at the pavement,
saying, "Thank you, I can see it clearly now."

"Mrs. Gates," Billy stuttered. "Mrs. Gates."

The chauffeur tried to block us, but she said,
"That's all right, Andrew. They're just kids. I'm
        safe."

"Our grandpa says hello," I blurted out.

She paused for half a beat, glanced at Billy,
then peered at me as if to study terror,
smiling. "Well I'll be damned. And who's he?"

"Don't listen to him," Billy said. "He's nuts."

"George McCracken," I said, "the one you spooned with
down by the railroad tracks."

                        "George McCracken."
She straightened, looked up at the strip of sky.
"Spooned. Well, that's one way to talk about it."
She laughed from deep down in her husky lungs.
"Old Georgie McCracken. Is he still alive?

Too scared to come downtown and say hello?"
She reached out from her furs and touched my hair.
"Thanks for the message, little man. I knew him.
I knew he'd never get out of this town.
You tell your grampa Hi from Liddy Carter."

The man at her elbow said they had to leave.
She nodded, handing her award and purse
to the chauffeur.

               Then flashbulbs started popping.
I saw her face lit up, then pale and caving
back into the darkness. "Christ," she whispered,
"get me out of here."

               I stumbled, or was pushed.
My eyes kept seeing her exploding at me,
a woman made entirely of light
beside the smaller figure who was real.
Two men tipped her into the limousine
and it slid off like a shark, parting the crowd.

        *

A picture ran in the next day's *Herald*—
the great actress touches a local boy.
For two weeks everybody talked about me,
but I kept thinking, "Is he still alive?
Too scared to come downtown and say hello?"

I thought of her decaying on a screen,
her ribs folding like a silk umbrella's rods,
while all the men who gathered around her
clutched at the remnants of her empty dress.

LONG LIFE

I.

Her white house on a hill, a barn, a meadow
leased to a neighbor who kept an old mare,
beyond her garden plot a field gone fallow,
and in the kitchen playing solitaire
her husband who moved slowly and was deaf,
rain-streaked dust on the mud room's window—
for me it all became another life,
as if my suburban life had met its shadow.
And she, the woman we called Auntie Wright,
who always smelled of baking, knew when cherries
were to be picked, or how to keep off blight,
held those lives together with her stories
told in a voice that had lost all trace of rage
in anticipation of a loving judge.

II.

At ninety-eight she still cooked dinner enough
for a lumbercamp, placed dishes before us
like prayers for the living. The food of love
came out of her kitchen sauced with her stories.
In one, a farmer's wife foretold a death
by dealing her neighbor the Ace of Spades,

and soon regretted it; within a month
the neighbor's boy died working in the woods.
A cousin in the Navy battled drink
and knocked a shot glass from a sailor's fist,
later to be thanked by the repentant drunk.
God was economical, and would waste
fewer than He saved. When she said Grace
the years of trouble vanished from her face.

III.

At a hundred and two she showed, at last, her age,
and let them take her to the nursing home.
Mind and body braced for her final siege.
When I visited, she could recall my name,
but, her blue eyes swimming in another time,
she also spoke the name of my dead brother.
I was the only guest within the room
and couldn't bring myself to interfere,
listened as the pieces of her past
were fretted into the sheets by her thin hands.
She knew that she had lived too long, and missed
the faces of her lost husband and friends;
her mind rose from the pillow as if caught
between their voices and the one I had brought.

IV.

I left the nursing home in a borrowed car,
drove through a town I hardly recognized
because I did not live there any more,
and trying not to think of her, I cruised
south toward Seattle on Interstate 5.
But I had heard her broken memory
and how she wished that she were not alive.
I felt the century inside of me
withering and lonely. She had come here
before the sinking of the Maine, before
Wilson at Versailles, prohibition, Lindbergh. . . .
I saw the black hole of her barn door
and smelled the dampness there among the tools,
the silent place that nobody controls.

BLACKENED PEACHES

I.

One fall it was Jim and me living out
to the county. We were farmers then. A cold
northeasterly blew down like a sheet of ice,
nipped the peach trees so the leaves turned black.
All winter long the leaves was black as could be.
They never dropped, not even when it snowed,
and it scared me some to walk under the boughs,
the way they rattled so unnaturally.

We were married years when that happened. I first
come out here from Wisconsin on the train—
1902, when I was a little red-head.
I remember the train stopped in the Cascades
and I saw all the mountain sheep in the world
was crossing the tracks. You wouldn't see that now.
A man named Slaughter met the train, shouting,
"This way to the Slaughter-house!" My father said
he meant a hotel, but I was never sure.
People have been dying on me ever since.

Soon after we moved up here to Nooksack
Father passed on. I went down with a fever
and that was when Doctor Hale first come to me.

He was a tall man, not a scary one,
and you could tell he was refined. He combed
his hair back neat, wore wire glasses that looked
tiny on a man so big, always wore
a suit and carried his black leather case.
His wife I believe died five years before,
but you saw no sign of sadness in him.
Once he asked me what was my favorite fruit
and I said, "Peaches," and the next visit, why,
there was a good ripe peach waiting for me.
He called me Sally Peaches with a laugh.

On my sixteenth birthday Doctor Hale come by
in his buggy with a bucket to make ice cream.
Halfway through our party Mama left the room.
Doctor Hale and I sat in the kitchen,
him with his hands on his knees, looking shy.
After a while he took his glasses off,
rubbed them with his handkerchief. His eyes was tired.
"Sally Peaches," he said. "You're too big for that.
I promise I won't baby you again."

He brought a box in from his buggy for me:
"I think, Sally, you're old enough for this."
The most beautiful party dress I ever saw
lay inside with its lace sleeves open to me.
Doctor Hale said he'd been saving it for years.
"I can tell it's going to fit you perfectly."

The next time I was over to town I walked
right by his office. I heard an axe's sound
from his yard, tip-toed up to have a look.
There was Doctor Hale stripped to the waist
except for his specs and braces, swinging
that axe as if he were a younger man.
When he paused to wipe his brow I could see
he looked angry, tired, or not right with himself;
he seemed to want to tear those logs apart
with bare hands. I left before he saw me,
but that night I kept seeing him, the way
all gentleness went out of him when he swung.

One day, though nobody was sick, he come
again to our house. Mother left us alone
and Doctor Hale stood awkwardly and looked
down at me through his lenses. We were quiet
so you could hear the rain clap on the roof.
I give him a flower from the kitchen vase;
he fingered it like something that was ill.
"Sally," he said, "tell me what I look like."
He smiled strangely and I suppose I blushed
and couldn't raise my eyes to look at him.
"No," he said. "I know how I look. I look old,
old enough to have been tired out working when
your father was sick. I never told you that
because I held some rather strange ideas.
You know, of course, I'm very fond of you."
He coughed at the flower in his spotted hands.

"But I developed these peculiar ideas.
What I mean is that now you're growing up.
You've had a lonely childhood in some ways,
but you're a woman and you'll marry soon
and then with luck you'll never be alone.
I'm wishing you good luck, good health. . . all good."
Each word he spoke then seemed to weaken him,
and when he drove away I sat there crying
though I couldn't tell my mother what it meant.

II.

I was only seventeen when I met Jim.
He lumberjacked in the camp out to the lake.
I always liked the woods, so green and nice,
the ferns in bunches, trees covered with moss.
When I was little I was scared to walk
alone for fear the Indians would get me,
but Jim made the woods seem lighter than before.
His family was Welsh. They all was singers.
Next to Doctor Hale you'd think he was small,
more my size, but he was a strong camp boss.
Men always said he was good to work for.
Once he let his whiskers grow like the men
and I thought they was awful-looking things.
"What's the matter, Sally?" says he. "Seen a ghost?"
"Jim," I says, "you've ruined your face."
                                   "Ruined?"
I told him I wouldn't stand for any man

who looked like a porcupine. That day he shaved.
He had wavy black hair and shiny eyes,
could eat like a mule and still dance all night.
He used to say there was music in the Welsh
and fight in the Norse—that's the stock I come from.
Jim was always a truthful husband, and I
told him only the one white lie. I said
my father used to call me Sally Peaches.
I suppose I wanted Jim to call me that,
but it never felt right when he said the name.

Then one year that northeasterly come down.
We'd been on the farm a while; Jim bought the place
so I wouldn't have to cook in a camp.
There was peach trees on it just for me, he said.
The cold he caught in that storm turned bad,
sank down in his lungs and worked there rasping him
with pain. I sent a neighbor for Doctor Hale
and all day sat with a fear he wouldn't come.
Finally I heard his buggy—he never
in his life would drive a car—stop outside,
and saw him stoop to come in at the door.
He went to work while I stayed in the kitchen
brewing tea. Outside the leaves was blackened,
rattling in the wind like sick men breathing.
Made me dizzy just to think of it.

When Doctor Hale come out he was pasty and old.
He took his glasses off, rubbed a sore spot

on the bridge of his nose, give me a flat look.
He said, "Jim's been asking for Sally Peaches."
There we were in the kitchen, six feet apart
and silent as frost on the windowpanes.

The black leaves was death, though. I knew for sure
they would take someone. That year Mama died.
That year, while the trees was still all blighted,
Doctor Hale was killed. His horse took a fright
out on Mountainview Road, pulled his buggy
off a bridge, and threw him into the river.
There's foxes on the road; people suppose
it was the foxes give that horse such a scare.

You never saw so big a funeral
as his. The church spilled people into the street.
The paper said a whole era was gone;
he was the last of the gentleman doctors.

III.

You won't believe me, but I saw him again.
I promise I saw him here in this room
twenty-two years ago, the year Jim died.
It wasn't too long after Kennedy
that Jim took sick again and I could see
the blood draining out of his face, his lips
a pale purple, skin damp and hands ice-cold.

I did the only thing I knew to do
and prayed to God not to take him away.

It was dark. The house rattled in a wind.
I sat there in the kitchen by the stove
muttering this prayer, and the room changed.
I knew I wasn't alone any more.
I turned and saw a man beside the door,
knew him by the wire rims of his glasses,
his smile peaceful though he was covered with rain.
I heard his voice with so much gentleness:
"Sally, all of our illnesses will end."
When he said my name it was like the sound
grew inside me till the tears had to fall.
I could almost feel his hand on my hair.
By the time I dried my eyes he was gone.

For eight long months Jim wasted away.
I remember cursing God for what he did
and I know in his heart how Jim cursed God.
Sometimes I wanted Doctor Hale to come,
but the dead can't be faithful any more.
I got up in the middle of the night
to give Jim his pills. Already it was like
I lived alone in a house with voices.

One of those nights I saw he'd gone at last.
I didn't know what to do. I didn't know
why I thought there was one more thing to do,

a last thing, because Jim was Welsh and I knew
there was something you had to do for the Welsh.
I thought about how fine he used to look.
How his eyes was bright. How he sang at camp.
I looked out the window and could feel him
lying there in the cold bed at my back.
I knew what he was telling me, and left
the window open for his soul to go.

III

DISCLOSURE

With blue official flap and legalese
the state acknowledges an end to what
began in privacy, in passing glances.
What I remember of your voice is not
an issue lawyers willingly address,
and I've avoided their neat document.
There was a time when the word "wife" warmed me,
but as you say I think too much of words.

Many nights I raised my head from the pillow,
watched you sleeping, wife in a girl's flannel,
there by the bed your window open.
Long-stemmed, unnamable flower in whom
I was lost and saved for ten brief years,
my rancor can't contain these images:
your hair lightened to its roots by Greek sun,
my maps of married pleasure on your skin.

It's strange what we can make ourselves believe.
Memory saves; recrimination uses
every twisted syllable of the past.
Still, with all the errors I acknowledge
added to those I fail or refuse to see,
I say our marriage was a gentle thing,
a secret bargain children sometimes make
and then forget when the weather's changed.

Lawyers put it another way; they don't know
how small exchanges still take place, of gifts
collected long ago, drawings of a house
we lived in, letters from friends we haven't told.
How separately we stumble on some object,
a book I signed, a scarf you knitted,
and call to tell the other it is there,
wondering if it will be wanted back.

SUMMER NIGHTS

Facing opposite, our childhoods back
to back, a continent between, we couldn't
possibly have guessed each other's lives.
Your lake, Ontario, was larger than
my Sound. The air at your horizon flapped
in summer heat. You saw the last gull flash
its 'm' across the gloaming, the last light
bleed from the copper beech, a taut sail
arc into the night. All this was native to you;
even a distanced vision of the poor
who came from the city to stroll the pier.
Yachts on the Genesee appeared to dance,
music mingled from the bars and clubs,
and even you, a girl from this neighborhood
of houses by the shore, might possibly escape.
One day your father took you sailing out
so far that land was sunken like a lost ship.
Later, a boyfriend's hand printing your dress,
you felt the radio tune your quivering nerves,
its voices caught like a streetlamp in the trees.

THE NEXT PLACE

for W.B.

She was from a town up north
that dug its own foundations out
and sold the coal to steel mills.
Slag heaps stood like old sores
on the ground's rump. That spring I kept
my wagon parked at the edge of town.
Curious women found me there,
complained of warts, distended livers,
spinal irritations of the kind
that interfered with work. Some came
childless, some to sell a caul,
believing in what I bought or sold.
Good people, I have often thought,
except when they run out of town.

One day when I worked a small crowd
near the river bank, I saw her;
next she bought a bottle I'd sworn
gave women skin like Cleopatra's.
She had a way of eyeing me
that saw through each of my tricks.
When she joined the crowd I weighed
my words like a grocer weighing pears,

added lines I'd never used before
about my years in Africa:
"This tale is not for tender ears,
though it's true as any Jesus told.
I know a tribe where women cook
hyena dung and rabid bats
and smear the tincture on their bosoms.
It keeps them young and foils the asp."
I saw her laughing, yet beguiled.

That night when the others left she stayed.
I said the cottonwoods were slaves,
broad Nubians fanning us
with fronds. The evening shadows stretched,
the river lulled our conversation.
I confessed I was theatrical,
a sinner if she wished, and she
rewarded candor with a kiss.
We left before they ran me out.

Now and then we catch word
of her folks as it blows past; I hear
her daddy's posted a reward
to any man who'd flay my hide,
but I'd swear before a jury
hell-bent on hanging me, she chose
to come, dance on my boards and lure
the strangers to our audience.
In towns like Wagon Mound, Raton,

Cuchara, Stonewall, Trinidad,
we've sold the good folk any dream
they'd buy.

       LaVeta, Aguilar,
Mosca, Moffat, Villa Grove,
always a move ahead of the law,
faster than preachers with the word.
For a year or so we've owned the moon,
I've tipped my hat to pinyon trees,
she's curtseyed to a fox,
and when we pass some mining town
the sooted stares don't bother us.
Sometimes she looks away from our fire,
forgets to tend the coffee pot,
and I, the wagon, blankets—all
of it empties from her gaze.
Maybe one night when I'm snoring
in my bed she'll rise and run
home, or to some stranger's camp,
tell of kidnapped gypsy life
and lies that carried her away;
maybe she'll have her own lies to tell
in towns I've never heard of.

THE CATCH

She is the one who never seems to suffer,
  dances brilliantly through the room
and, only to lost men, appears to offer
  smiles mistaken for a home.

Now catch yourself before you think it's real,
  before the vulnerable gift,
and know that she's determined not to feel,
  although she will accept a lift.

Catch yourself, and realize you're a bore
  to anyone who's that much younger.
Don't burden her with all that you adore,
  or with your pitiable hunger.

LETTER FROM NEW YORK

Downstairs my neighbor and his lover
fight as if intent on murder;
floorboards pound and my body tenses,
expecting gunshots to break it up.

I wonder what returns me where
this littered, untenable street
dead-ends behind a hospital.
No one's dying yet, except

across the way. The periodic
scream of an ambulance unites
patients and doctors who otherwise
would never knowingly have met.

What caused our meeting weeks ago
must have been an equal need. There
in Colorado we drove west
suspended in a freezing fog;

the high plains to either side
became mere emanations—
grass and fences swimming past
in a sea of sunlit whiteness.

The car held us like a humming shell,
chasing the road's receding line
until fog broke on a row of peaks,
blue and solidly before us.

The plane tilted when I left,
allowing me to see the snow
endlessly unbroken—a promise
few of us seem equal to.

The killers below apologize
and right the toppled furniture.
One of them puts on a record,
as if its dreaminess could heal.

POSTSCRIPT

Chilling as gardens in old nursery rhymes,
this weather stunts the crocus, leaving mud
and rainwater's dull, suburban sheen.
The mood I have entered upon leaving you
is worse than grief; I am the villain here,
you the injured child who will not let me in.
I'd swear we imagined this, but the cold
hardens my blood, insensible as stone.

IN THE PHYSIC GARDEN

Though at a confluence of neighborhoods,
it's easily missed. North, a housing project
abuts the Genesee. Then traffic surges
between a block of genteel houses and
a famous cemetery's strata—the dead
have their pretensions too, durable as stone.
I thought of this junction of disparate hopes
the other day, walking here with you
and a man who had been your lover years before.

A sort of outdoor gallery of herbs
perserved within a screen of oaks and conifers,
this is an immigrant's dream of the Old World
probably as it never was, the grey
stone folly lording over its grotto:
walls where secret meetings might take place,
where even the cracked masonry, the lovers'
initials scratched under an arch, conspire.
There is a round shrub once shaped like a heart.

But that seemed part of another privacy.
Instead of watching you I bent and read:
coltsfoot is a sovereign cure for asthma,
celandine for sore eyes, ringworm and warts
(it is also helpful in removing teeth).

Rosemary strengthens the memory, rue
combats unconsciousness, headaches, nosebleeds,
and the yellow cowslip, good with palsy and pimples,
works wonders for a mad dog's bite.

We laughed at all that admirable quaintness.
For me the words themselves are remedies
because so nearly forgotten. The builders,
for all I know, were sentimentalists,
wanting a place where no one chooses sides
and what one cherishes still has no name.
That you and a former lover could be friends,
that I could love your past because it made you,
were granted in this artificial garden.

A MAP OF SCOTLAND

Your hands were eloquent, tracing
the immigrant's sea-route back
to disembark a child again
and find Glengarnock as it was:
the forge, your father's apiary. . . .

Inland from Largs, past all the laws,
it is a place the map remembers.
Trains can go there, but it is gone
as you knew it in that other life
before you came to America.

The row houses of your childhood street
were all leveled some time ago.
It would be years before your father
confessed to his homesickness, years
before you ventured back to look.

But there are lives too full for telling
even if we could see them clearly.
When I met you I watched your hands
lightly touching the folds of paper,
so near to mine it made me tremble.

CHAUTAUQUA

I.

The summer village lay behind its gate,
a jumble-sale of architectural styles
with a little park shaped like the Holy Land.
Empty now. We were its only tourists.
We walked for hours, each corner an excuse
to go on talking, even when it rained
and we leaned together under the bent spokes
of the hotel keeper's sad, black umbrella.

At one point, lost in a farmer's marshy woods,
it didn't matter if we found the car
or returned to the confusing charm behind
Chautauqua's gate. There was much to notice, much
to talk about, describing circles there,
and all those awkward circles from the past.

II.

Isn't it always what we want to believe,
that we could send fear away in a letter,
that each word it contains is a new body
opened to the body of another's word?

Our bodies touching, the fit of skin and fur.
Whether the snow deepened outside the window,
or whether there was a window in the room,
there is still this willingness, the nip and tuck

that makes believing pagans of us, searching
the crossed A's, the loops and you's of letters
for a sign, a further confirmation.
The laughter echoes what the flesh affirmed.

And will affirm. There is always that hope:
places on the border between here and there,
the border where two beds are pushed together,
crossed at all hours under the shared blankets.

III.

Easter. The thick rain erupts like laughter,
a melancholy rumble at first, then
sheer hysteria sweeping the street below.
The birds squeal like monkeys in wet branches
as if to say THE LONG DROUGHT IS OVER!
THE CITY HAS BEEN SAVED!

Small dun-colored swallows, they've been away
the whole relentless winter,
Like them we can no longer call ourselves
both honest and young. But I assume they know
what it's like to be lost in endless circles
and, suddenly weightless, sense which way to fly.